How to Plan a Wedding on a Budget

The Ultimate Guide to Planning a Wedding on a Budget

by Gabriella Reznik

Table of Contents

Introduction

So, you and your significant other have decided to take that glorious step to matrimony. You have your hearts a-flutter from the excitement of your impending nuptials. But the thought of the titanic costs behind every gorgeous wedding you've attended or heard about keeps dampening your collective spirits.

Have No Fear! The Mystical Wedding Budgeter is here!

In this book, I'll take you through all the little tips and tricks that allow financially-astute brides and grooms to have their beautiful wedding, at a fraction of the average cost. Some of these require creative, out-of-the-box thinking, while many others are simply achieved by meeting your expectations in unexpected places. Most of these, however, are tips that the myriad of services and agents specializing in wedding-related work would never advise you on; for the simple reason that their incomes would diminish if most weddings started following these guidelines.

So, are you ready? Let's get started!

Chapter 1: Define Your Budget (Draw the Line Without Breaking Bank)

The first mistake many people make when they start planning is that they want to list everything they can think of to include in their wedding, and then just accept the sum total of the costs as their budget. The problem with that is that the cost of weddings could run from anywhere between $1,000 (yes, these figures for weddings do exist, and beautiful ones at that) to $25,000 and above, easily.

If you first make a list of the things you want and then decide your total budget, it leads to panic, disappointment and chagrin when you realize that you can't possibly cover it all. It leads to questions of loans to cover the costs of the list that you first made. Many people have the absurd notion that having to compromise on your wedding's expenses will make it seem second-rate. But do you really want to start a life of marital bliss with loans and debts hanging over your heads? If possible, stay away from them altogether. If not, then minimize the loan amount as much as you can. While it may not cover everything you may have wished for in your wedding, the future 'you' will thank you for not piling debt-stress on your day-to-day lives just for the sake of adding more baubles & trinkets (that you could have done without) on that one day.

I should point out here that the first two chapters of this book will likely be a part of the same conversation. However it's better to have a concrete monetary figure in mind, which both of you can afford, before you start listing everything you'd like to include in your wedding. Hopefully the validity of this point can be proven by this question- When you think about buying a house, do you decide on a budget first and then check which offers meet your requirements, or do you first check out everything from studio apartments to palaces before discussing the budget? If you put in that effort for a matter which impacts your residential arrangements, an indubitably longer-lasting decision, why shouldn't that apply to a single celebration as well, even if that is your wedding?

You should first sit with your partner, get a no-nonsense idea of where the both of you stand financially, including present loans, debts, collective income, monetary gifts from relatives (if any), and so on and so forth.

Next, you need to set a ceiling for the maximum you could afford to spend on your wedding, without breaking the bank or having to suffer for it in the coming future. Remember that happiness in marriages is determined by what happens after the wedding, not by how grandiose the day itself may have been. In fact, financial instability is one of the leading causes of friction in marriages. Don't pile that on your own head.

If you have savings, don't blow them all. Remember that your lives need to go on after your wedding day as well. If you still think that you can afford to take out a loan, calculate the amount that you could afford to re-pay every month without cutting into essential costs like utilities, living expenses etc., then check credit offers for an amount that suits your requirements.

The harsher you are with yourself here, as unromantic as this may sound, the more you'll thank yourself later.

Once you've arrived at a budgetary sum, remember that at least 5-10% of that money should remain unassigned. This is simply to prepare you for any unexpected eventualities that you may face before or on the wedding day, and to ensure that solving the problem doesn't put you over the budget.

The monetary sum which the two of you arrive at here is now your line in the sand. Many people draft a budget and then constantly exceed it, through self-delusions like 'We're already spending so much, what harm could a little more do?' The point here is that the budget is meaningless if you don't at least try to stick to it. If you didn't think that a little more could have harmed you to begin with, it should have been included in your first budget draft. If anything, your efforts should be aimed at shaving more off of that initial budget amount, rather than exceeding it in any way.

Now that the two of you have a maximum figure in mind (that won't break your bank), we can move on to the next part. Congratulate yourselves at this point, because you've made things much easier from here on out. I promise you that the rest of the decisions that you need to make, including prioritizing, compromising, bargaining, etc. will be far easier to handle now that you know where your spending limit is capped.

Chapter 2: Compare Your Dream Weddings (Prioritize the "Must-Haves")

Now we move on to the second important part of the first step in planning your beautiful wedding. As I mentioned before, these two chapters will likely be a part of the same conversation between you and your partner.

First, both of you need to sit down separately and write out everything you've ever wanted to include in your wedding, whether it was something you encountered at a friend's wedding, saw in a magazine, on TV, or something you thought about on your own. While men may or may not have strong opinions about wedding-related matters, it's important that both of you participate in this exercise and at least write down what does matter to you individually.

You need to list down every detail that may occur to you: dates, venues, food, music, décor, photographers, flowers, seasonal preferences and any other smaller details. You should also mention beside each point exactly how important it would be for you to have that element, i.e. 'Absolutely must-have', 'Would prefer to have but would settle for an alternative', 'Would like to have but not a necessity', etc. If you want, you can develop a scale of 1 to 10 (1 = not very important, but would be nice….. & …… 10 = absolutely must have) to make the list organization easier.

An important point to mention here is that if your list is full of notes saying 'must-have', you're not doing this exercise as seriously as you think. The only true must-have on the day is your partner beside you during the ceremony. Remember to keep perspective.

Once the two of you have completed your lists, swap them and read through your partner's list on your own first, before getting together and comparing them. Do not judge the other's preferences or comment on the other's list until you can talk through it together.

After you have read each other's lists, sit down together and write down all the 'must-have's of both in a new fresh list. Unless your 'not a necessity's are on your partner's 'must-have' list, then cut them out altogether. Discuss each of the 'prefer to have's to see which ones can you cut out on your own, or through some compromises between the two of you. Once you've done that, write down the remaining elements below the 'must-have's on the fresh list.

Now comes the hardest part. The two of you need to sit with that fresh list, and re-assign 'must-have's for both of you. Re-assign priorities to each of the elements based on how you feel about them as a couple. If your partner has no opinion about a particular detail, while you think it may be a 'must-have', the two of you can still talk it out together and prioritize it as a 'must-have'. I can certainly promise you that having your budget in mind while you're discussing all of this will make it so much simpler to make decisions and assign practical priorities to these elements, rather than having to go through it the other way around.

After you've finished this process, pat yourselves (or each other) on the backs once again. You've already saved yourselves a lot of money, while still retaining the most important elements that you want in your wedding ceremony. From here on out, this guide and your guile will be the most important tools in helping you cross that finish line to matrimony without having to feel like Atlas - carrying a sky-sized debt on your shoulders for the foreseeable future.

Chapter 3: Your Guest List (AKA the "Black Hole" in Your Budget)

Nothing, I repeat, absolutely nothing affects your expenditures like your guest list. The total cost of every item on your list takes this figure into account – size of venue, food, drinks, cutlery, place settings, decorations, invitations, party favors etc. So give yourselves a break. After spending so much time trying to curb your expenses in a hundred different ways, don't let this list rule you, sucking up all your money like a financial black hole.

As I mentioned before, the only 'must-have's on the day of your wedding are you and your Significant Other. Besides, your wedding day is not a circus. It's not a show to put on for the sake of networking, and it certainly isn't a day for politeness to take charge. It's far too expensive an affair to worry about imagined slights and personal/professional politics. Your wedding celebrations are the last place in which you should be compromising on the emotional quality of your guests and company, just to be a people pleaser.

Really, what kind of a day would you prefer? One where you spend all your time being pulled one way or another by people you barely know, remember, or like; all the while having to keep an exhaustingly polite smile? Or a day where the only people you have around you are the ones who know and love the both of you, who understand what you mean to each other and what this moment truly signifies for you, and who exude unadulterated joy, love and warmth in the face of the proceedings?

When you and your partner finally sit down to discuss the guest list, first discuss whether each of you wants a small or a large wedding, and why. Once you have a better idea of what your partner wants, and their reasons behind it, it becomes far easier to determine whether those reasons are worth the money that the two of you would collectively spend bringing those visions to fruition.

When you start working on this list, first note down the people that you absolutely, unequivocally want at your wedding, i.e. yourselves, your immediate family, and your closest friends (whether personal or professional). From within this short list, containing all your near and dear ones, create your wedding party.

Only once you've completed this portion of the exercise should you move on to the rest of the guests. From here on out, be extremely critical with yourselves for every name that you add to the invitational record. If you have any second-cousins that you're close to, or their parents, invite them and them alone. You also have the choice of not inviting anyone beyond immediate family members if you don't want to be seen to be playing favorites. Under no circumstances should you invite your entire extended family just so that you can have the three or four people out of them all that you really want at your wedding. The moment you start doing that, your guest list will explode beyond your control.

Also, remember that people are quite aware of how expensive a wedding can be nowadays. There's no shame in simply explaining that to any relative or colleague you couldn't invite, after the wedding is done. As long as you're upfront about this motive, most people will understand. The ones who don't, who take umbrage even though they weren't close enough to you to make your A-list, were looking for a reason to be annoyed with you anyway, and should definitely not be partaking in one of the happiest moments of your life.

Keep in mind that the shorter your guest list, the more effectively you can use your allocated money to throw a grander celebration - if you choose to do so. –This is far better than having a comparatively subdued affair because you were hosting 100-200 people on a budget that was stretched thin. The added advantage is that the ones participating in this grand celebration will only be the people you love the most and who care about you beyond a shadow of a doubt – basically, the people you'd want to give a grand time to anyway.

These are the pointers you should keep in mind while finalizing your guest list:

1. The shorter the list, the better the party and atmosphere.

2. Don't spend time obsessing over equal numbers from both sides.

3. Don't invite anyone with whom you don't have an emotional attachment.

4. Don't invite anyone simply to be polite, especially if it's only because you're inviting someone they're related to or friends with. It's far easier to give a heartfelt explanation or apology later, if you feel like they're entitled to one, than to spend hundreds of dollars trying to be a people pleaser.

Chapter 4: Basic Starter Tips Before You Step Out

By this point, you and your partner have finished every step that you could accomplish before setting out to bring your plans to life. At this juncture, before you start talking to different vendors, agencies and contractors, there are a few pointers you should keep in mind.

1. Do not engage the services of wedding planners if you can help it.

Wedding planners are essentially middle-agents with established networks who plan and materialize the vision of a wedding, as laid out by them or the couple. Either way, most charge a hefty fee for their services, and are not particularly driven to get you the cheapest alternatives, the most creative solutions, or the best bargains. This is especially true since the survival of their network partly relies on them bringing business to their regular affiliates.

By planning your wedding yourselves, you maintain control over every cent that you spend and every negotiation that it takes to make it all happen, without having to spend extra money from your tight budget on a third-party. Of course, if you have a friend who is a wedding planner, take their advice, and let them tag along from time-to-time. But never give up control over your wedding-related matters. Absolutely no one will be as motivated to get you the best outcome, in keeping with your vision, as you and your partner will.

2.   Haggle, compare, and haggle some more.

The best way to make the most of your money is never to get sucked into the pace of a business you're trying to hire for your wedding. Understand that, as the consumer, you drive the market. You hold the money. Remember that in every negotiation you undertake, they need your money more than you need their business. For every conceivable purpose, there are at least a hundred others who will do the same job.

One of the more disturbing social trends is that people are beginning to consider haggling impolite or rude. It's neither. Haggling has been a basic, accepted business practice since time immemorial. Companies haggle over each cent of a share during mergers or take-overs; businessmen haggle upwards to earn as much as they can from each customer. Financially-shrewd men and women face no trouble in accepting the art of haggling to be a part of their every-day lives, wherever they can, which is why they manage their money far better than others. After all, budgeting and money-management is as much about keeping your money, and maximizing its potential returns, as it is about incomes, investments and other such avenues.

Whenever you ask a business for a quote, haggle it as far down as you can. After doing this, go out and compare the lowest rates that they can offer you with other businesses that provide the same service or product. Use the lowest rates from each company that you haggle with to further lower the rates on the next one you deal with, and watch competitive market pricing do its magic. Haggle, compare, and haggle some more till you're sure you've got the best quotes for each service or product that you need for your wedding. Each cent will count, and the sense of accomplishment and empowerment that you'll feel after each successful negotiation will make it all worthwhile.

Another ploy for haggling that I recommend is asking a firm or service to lower their prices in exchange for placing their business cards in a box by the entrance, or at some other such place at your wedding venue. Since weddings are not repeat-business by nature, most wedding-related firms rely heavily on referential customers. The less well-known the firm that you're dealing with, the more effectively this ploy should work.

3. The mere mention of weddings increases the price a few notches.

This is a logical and universally-known truth, yet few consumers ever capitalize on it. Businesses that rent tents for all occasions are often visibly cheaper than others who peddle the same quality product but exclusively deal with weddings. Regular caterers are often cheaper, with better food, than a lot of wedding caterers. It's the curse of the 'Wedding premium' pricing.

The kernel of wisdom here is simple. Firstly, shun most businesses that exclusively deal with weddings. Search for other similar firms that don't gear their services exclusively to this particular demographic.

Secondly, if the firm that you're negotiating with doesn't need to know that they're dealing with a wedding in order to effectively provide their product, i.e. caterers, cutlery rentals, décor rentals, etc., don't mention it to them. Approach them and describe the services or items that you need, but say that it's for a party. Once they've given you a quote and you've haggled it down, you can then mention that it's for a wedding. Since they've already given you a quote for their products, they can't change their prices thereafter.

As an alternative, several web bloggers, commentators and their ilk also mention the charm of the 'secret elopement'. If you're approaching a business and absolutely have to mention that their services are required for a wedding celebration, say that you're secretly eloping, and thus are unable to foot normal prices out of your own pockets. This may get you no special treatment from the company at all, or it may get you a neat little discount that you wouldn't have gotten otherwise.

4. Don't underestimate the power of creative, unusual, out-of-the-box thinking.

Most people refuse to spend any extra time trying to find innovative ways of including elegance and grandeur in their nuptial celebrations, and they usually end up getting the same things that others have, from the same places that others do. The problem with that is that it's exactly how most weddings end up costing the newly-married couple an arm and a leg to foot the bills.

Just as examples: Once you've selected the style of wedding dress you like, go to sites like amazon.com and search for 'custom wedding dresses'. If you have the know-how to pick out a verified, trust-worthy seller (which is easy, and there are plenty of guides to supplement your knowledge on this), you can get gorgeous, brand-new, hand-made wedding dresses starting from $70 or below.

Or, instead of searching for caterers who'd supply the food for your wedding, at ridiculous costs-per-head, talk to the owner of your favorite local food-truck. They usually use seasonal ingredients, which makes the food taste better, fresher, and is lighter on the wallet. The truck can be parked right outside your wedding venue, with the kitchen churning out food through the celebration (which you know is yummy, and costs a lot less than the caterer would have charged you).

The point is, eschew the belief that traditional is better, or that something established for purpose A cannot be used for purpose B. Think out-of-the-box, and you will find more solutions to each problem than you'll know what to do with.

5. Carry cash for smaller transactions, to get better discounts.

This point should be self-evident. People prefer cash over credit cards or checks.

This is pretty useful for transactions smaller than your venue payments (but even here it may help in securing venues faster, with regards to deposits). If you're approaching caterers, photographers, etc. trying to haggle the price down, a final offer of cash payment, instead of a check, may get you a lower final price. However, try to avoid up-front cash-payments long before your wedding day. Instead, steer negotiations towards cash-payments after services rendered, if you can.

6. Use all the resources available to you, without guilt or unnecessary moral baggage.

If you have any friends, family, relatives etc. with any talents or skills that may prove useful during the planning or execution of your wedding, approach them!

Many couples try to avoid requesting help from near-and-dear ones since they want to prevent any inconvenience to others. The catch here is that anyone who cares about you would love to contribute in any way they can, adding value to the happiest day of your life rather than simply attending like so many others. Your need for assistance helps them feel closer and more important to you, and they will gladly render any services that would be able to lighten your load. So stop feeling guilty and being overtly and unnecessarily polite or formal with people who would gladly help if you but asked. If any of them have a reason that may prevent them from being able to help you, they'll inform you of it themselves either way. You lose absolutely nothing by asking.

And this particular point applies to everyone you come across, friends, family, firms, businesses, etc.: You'll only receive if you ask.

7. Absolutely everything is far cheaper in the off-season.

This one's obvious. Prices, packages and availabilities are always in your favor in the wedding off-season (November-March or so). Negotiations also work far better, and it's far cheaper to have much more opulent weddings, at these times. Even if you have your heart set on a date within the wedding season, usually for sentimental or reasons relating to seasonal preference, consider compromising into the off=season. Remember that you don't need to get married on a day that's already important to you. Whichever day you get married on will, by its very nature, be special from then on.

Every cent reduced from one expense is a cent available for another, better, more worthwhile option elsewhere.

Chapter 5: Photography and Vidcography

Before I start discussing the tips related to this chapter, let me mention one thing. If you believe your budget to be too limited to employ professionals for both photos and videos, always choose to spend on a photographer rather than on a video maker. Many people consider that videos will capture more, and therefore are a better investment. However, bear in mind that wedding videos are realistically watched perhaps a handful of times over the course of your life. Photos are invaluable and timeless. When was the last time you went to a friend's place, or to a relative's, and sat through their wedding videos? People rifle through wedding photos, their own and others', much more often.

Moving on to the meat of the matter, if you have a professional photographer in mind and you enjoy their work, approach them and try to haggle the price down. However, bear in mind that there are plenty of other approaches you can use as well.

If your local hobby centers have photography classes, or if a local school or college has a course on photography, you can approach the instructor of said class and try and get a quote from them with regards to their hiring cost for a wedding. They usually have portfolios of their work, which you can check out before hiring them. You may find professionals among them, who are usually as talented as established wedding photographers, but who are also cheaper and need the work more (giving you more leverage in negotiations).

As an alternative, some people also buy a lot of disposable cameras and place them on each table at their wedding, to inspire their guests to take as many pictures as they can and to therefore compile the couple's wedding album. In this case you can also ask the guests to scan and upload the photos that they've taken to a joint online album that you can create on photography sites, thus easing the load of work you need to do to sort through them all. However, bear in mind that most couples who have tried this approach found that a lot of guests don't bother with the cameras at all, and most photographs that they get from the ones who do are hardly worth keeping. Use this option at your own discretion, but it could be a fun idea.

You can also rope in a few of your friends whom you know to be decent or good amateur photographers (these people usually have good digital cameras, or you can borrow some from others and provide them if they don't), and assign them the role of capturing the memorable moments of your wedding.

As for videographers, I've already mentioned before that these are far less important that good photographs of your wedding. If you know a good videographer, and their services are cheap enough to include that expense in your budget, go ahead and hire them. However, there's another alternative that you can use to minimize this cost in your expenses.

Most digital cameras today, if not all, come with video options. If you know anyone who enjoys making home videos, or whom you know to be good at it, you can always ask them to become the official videographer of your wedding.

Or else, you can ask a couple of friends with good digital cameras to cover all the aspects of your wedding together. Once you've gotten all of the videos they make, you can always approach students or instructors in local cinematography classes, asking them to use and edit all that material to provide you with a single, good, polished, wedding video. They might happily do this for free, or at most for a small fee. They will likely find the experience more important. This offers the advantage of being able to view your wedding from several different vantage points, much like a movie. The multiple videographers will also be able to cover, and capture, far more content than a single team roaming around trying to shoot the whole thing.

Chapter 6: Music

Music, in weddings, is by far the easiest thing to arrange and solve. Most wedding DJs and live bands charge a hefty price for their services, yet it's not always the kind, quality, or choice of songs that you would prefer.

Invest instead in a good speaker system, either a cheap purchase or a rental one. Compile a list of all the music that you'd like to hear playing on your wedding day, and upload them all to an Mp3 player. Rope in a friend or relative to take care of the sound system, and operate the player as needed or requested. This gives you complete control over the kind of music that plays, without having to deal with the attitudes and preferences of over-priced, glorified, human disc-flippers.

If you want live music for the ceremony itself, you can always approach music instructors from small institutes, schools, colleges or hobby centers. These musicians have a ton of experience and are often as talented as wedding-orientated musical services, at a fraction of the price. They also often need the gig far more (again, leverage in price haggling). You can get a single harp-player or flautist to cover the live music for your wedding ceremony. They provide a quaint, peaceful, melodious backdrop to your service without having to deal with the hustle, clamor and expense of entire bands.

Another great way of providing a musical outlet for guests is to host an open-mic night on the day before your wedding.

Finally, you can also ask your photographer or caterer if they know any good musicians, using their reference to get you a discount.

Chapter 7: Food, Drinks, and Cake

Food and drinks provided at your celebrations is often one of the largest costs for you to consider, depending on the size of your guest list. Traditionally people try to provide two large meals during their wedding celebrations (usually three-course sit-downs) – one for the wedding itself and the other during the reception on the same evening. However, these are usually exorbitantly expensive, wasteful, and not always the best quality food that you could provide for your guests.

A lot of couples also report that plenty of food from the second meal is often wasted, since people are still full from the first; they end up wishing that they'd provided a single great meal instead.

You could consider converting your wedding meal to a brunch, thus saving a lot of money. You could provide an array of hors d'oeuvres instead of a proper meal, and provide a buffet later in the evening. You could sit down with the chefs employed under your caterer and work out a menu involving seasonal ingredients. Avoid all exotic products, since they're significantly more expensive.

Delicious, good-quality finger foods and appetizers like meat-balls, nuggets, etc. are often available for cheap in bulk at wholesalers and supermarkets, and you could buy these and provide them for your guests as food during the ceremony. If you go with this option and aren't satisfied with just that, you could also provide crowd pleasers like a cotton candy machine or a hot-dog stand that you could hire for the day as added options around your venue.

One option that I've previously discussed is approaching your favorite food-truck, instead of a caterer. They provide great food at a far cheaper price than most caterers. You could have their truck parked behind the venue, releasing tables a few at a time for people to go grab whatever food from the menu takes their fancy.

If you don't want people to get their own food you can employ a few students (or other such factions of the populace who are always strapped for cash) to act as servers instead.

The obvious extension of this point is that you can approach any local restaurants or eateries that you frequent and which you know the owners of through regular patronage. These should provide you with great packages for buffets, including rented silverware and other such cutlery, and you're likely already familiar with most of their culinary offerings. If you let them keep stacks of their take-away menus and other such paraphernalia next to the buffet table, they could also provide you with further discounts on the low priced-packages that they've already offered.

With drinks and alcohol, the first point worth mentioning is that you should always keep an open bar. Avoid cash-bars, where guests have to pay for each drink they take, at any cost. It leaves your guests with an unpleasant feeling, and dampens the emotional impact of the proceedings by seeming slightly money-hungry. If you wouldn't ask your guests to pay for their drinks when you invite them to your home, why would you do that at your wedding?

If you want to keep the costs of alcohol lower than they would otherwise have been, serve just wine and beer at your wedding celebrations. You can also add the option of one signature cocktail among the list of alcohols served. However, stay away from champagne altogether if you can, or just get a single bottle for the toast.

As an alternative, you could provide just one cocktail or alcoholic beverage, and serve a whole host of fruit-based or other non-alcoholic drinks at your wedding. You could even remove alcohol from the menu altogether.

Purchase your alcohol from wholesalers, not retailers. Discuss with them in advance whether you can bring back any unopened bottles for a refund.

If you're hiring a catering service to serve your meals and drinks make sure that you've asked them if they charge a corkage fee. Several catering firms charge a fee for every bottle of alcohol that they open during your celebrations, even if you've bought and provided the alcohol yourselves. You can discuss possible discounts, or even doing away with the corkage fee altogether, in your negotiations. As I've alluded to before, it's far better to just hire students to act as servers and bar-tenders, than to use wedding-oriented services.

As for cakes, it is best to simply get a small 1-pound or 1½-pound, double-tier cake for cutting after the ceremony, and buy sheet cake to serve to the guests. Many supermarkets provide cheap, good-quality cakes that you could serve to your guests instead of buying a large, expensive wedding cake to cut and serve to all.

If you have relatives or friends who would enjoy baking for you, you could create mounds of cupcakes that would be placed around the small celebration cake, and which would then be served to the guests instead of the cake. Options such as ice-cream cakes also work well with guests, and will still be a lot cheaper than a large cake from most wedding bakers.

Chapter 8: Dress and Apparel

The wedding dress is widely held to be the most important, element of the preparations for the bride. As such, it is often also the most stressful. While the fabric and labor that's gone into a dress wouldn't cost a fraction of the final price, designers and boutiques charge exorbitant prices based on their brand-name and the emotional relevance that their ware will hold for soon-to-be brides.

There are, however, plenty of alternative ways to get a gorgeous wedding dress without having to mortgage your home for it.

You should first get a clear idea of the design, cut and style of dress that you want. Once you understand the kind of dress that you want, sample sales, discount outlets, off-the-rack clearances and other such places can offer you far cheaper alternatives than boutiques and custom designers. If you do find your dress at a sample sale, make sure to check every stitch on the dress before you purchase it. Some dresses end up in sales simply because they're too damaged to be sold in other places. Alterations and corrections could end up exceeding the cost of the dress itself.

Another option that I've previously mentioned is checking online sites. There are plenty of re-seller websites that deal in beautiful dresses which have been worn once before. Websites like amazon.com (again, search for 'custom wedding dresses') list plenty of reliable businesses that provide gorgeous dresses for a fraction of the prices found elsewhere. The catch is that quite a few of these providers are based out of China. However the quality of their work is impeccable. If the seller is trust-worthy, they will have no troubles answering any barrage of questions that you may send their way before making a purchase. Always remember to check relevant taxation on import, as well as postage and delivery fees that would apply to your dress. You should then factor those into the final expense.

If you know cheap, reliable tailors, or are skilled in the sartorial arts yourself, you could buy a similar dress and alter it yourselves to suit your tastes. As for veils, it's far more practical to purchase the fabric and fashion the veil yourself, or enlist the help of a friend for this purpose. Alternatively, you could do away with the veil and sport a grand hair-do, or use seasonal flowers in your hair to add a touch of natural beauty instead of covering yourself with fabric.

For the groom's apparel, it is much better to invest in a simple suit that could be used after your wedding as well, rather than rent an expensive and unnecessary tuxedo.

For the bridesmaids, you could pick out cheap dresses or fabrics and ask them to fashion dresses along your directions. You could also just pick out dresses and ask them to pay for it themselves. It's not an unusual custom, and so you shouldn't feel any trepidation in doing so.

For the groomsmen and ushers, the best way to cut out any unnecessary expenditure would be to ask them to wear any suits or formal wear that they may have, making sure that they match in color. They can look sharply dressed without needing to blow a chunk of your money to make it happen. The boutonnieres for the males in the wedding party can be fashioned out of green leaves, or cheaper seasonal flowers, and can be easily hand-crafted by you and your friends, saving up a lot of money from your budget.

Chapter 9: Venue and Decorations

The venue for a wedding usually sets the tone and back-drop for the entire event, and people will therefore fight tooth-and-nail to reserve their dates in opulent wedding halls and grand hotel banquet rooms, ending up blowing a leviathan-sized chunk of their budget doing so.

Keep this in mind – absolutely any venue can turn into a beautiful matrimonial setting, with the right work put into it. Give preference to venues where you can hold the wedding ceremony and reception at the same location, or at least within walking distance. It cuts out any transportation expenses on your behalf for your guests and wedding party, and provides a quaint, old-world feel when the entire gathering headed by the wedding party can have a pleasant walk between the two venues.

Instead of going for the same-old wedding halls, try searching for townhouses and villas in your near or slightly distant surroundings that provide rented spaces for parties and celebrations. These usually have outdoor spaces as well, and thus can double up as a venue for your wedding and the reception together.

There are plenty of old churches which provide venues for weddings at little to no cost. You could also approach schools for use of their gyms, or less expensive clubs for the use of their grounds.

A popular venue among couples who want a beautiful wedding on a tight budget seems to be state and local parks. Many of these have beautiful kiosks, lake-side or otherwise, which serve as a breath-taking location for weddings. If you're choosing an outdoor venue though, make sure that bad weather doesn't lay waste to your plans. Several of these parks have some kind of enclosure that would suit the purposes of a wedding perfectly.

A lot of wedding venues come with their own caterers, lighting equipment, etc. Make sure you've asked every relevant question to make sure that there aren't any such restrictions or hidden costs. Also, remember that the order of pricing for venues in a week starts with the highest costs on Saturdays > Sundays > Fridays > any other day of the week.

Websites like rentalhq.com often come in handy to get in touch with contractors for wedding set-ups, and to get an idea of potential venue-related costs.

Venue decorations can easily be done by you, your friends and relatives together. Buy cheap seasonal flowers from wholesalers, instead of the expensive traditional ones, in order to reduce this extortionate cost. You can arrange the flowers yourselves, using alternative setting options like glass mason-jars instead of vases. Add more leafy twigs, or branches with seasonal berries (which are significantly cheaper), to add touches of beauty with a twist, instead of buying truck-loads of expensive flowers for one day.

Also consider making paper lanterns as center-pieces, instead of traditional options. They're extremely easy and fun to make, and the only cost involved would be the paper. If you know anyone adept at calligraphy, you could ask them to write you and your partner's names in a beautiful script on the sides of the lanterns, keeping a small candle in the middle of each of them, for a charming and unorthodox piece of décor.

For place-settings, the easiest way to add personalized glamor to your wedding is to go to a beach and collect shells, or collect small, smooth rocks from wherever you may, and write the names of the guests on them with paint or markers, instead of spending large amounts of money on getting them printed.

If you aren't particularly gifted in hand-crafting decorations, you always have the option of going to sites like Amazon and buying cheap decorations from there that you and your loved ones could put up together. In such cases, you can also re-sell the decorations at half-price on the same sites after your wedding celebrations are over, thus re-acquiring some of the money that you spent.

While renting the chairs, tables, etc. for your wedding, do not bother renting chair-covers. This and other such small details are quite often wholly unnecessary, and their absence is never missed by the guests. Stick to necessities, saving your money for other last-minute weather-related, or problematic considerations.

Chapter 10: Miscellaneous Components (Invitations, Favors, Gift Registry, Officiant, Save-the-Dates, Etc.)

Betrothed couples often spend a lot of money getting invitations designed by a professional wedding designer, and even more getting them printed and embossed on thick paper after that.

Avoid going to professional designers altogether. If you can do it yourself, or know someone who can do it for you, use that option and save the pointless expense. Alternatively, there are countless 'Wedding Invitation' templates that are available for download online, and which only need a few minutes of tweaking to match your needs perfectly. A personal printer only needs minor adjustments in settings to print on thicker paper, providing a fast, cheap option when compared to going to a professional invitation designer and printer.

If you have your design ready but don't have any printing options available to you, approaching a simple printing service would still save you a lot of money as compared to firms that deal in wedding invitations. If possible, you can also approach your work-place and ask if their printers could be made available to you for the purpose of printing your wedding invitations.

Send your Save-the-dates via e-mail or other online free-mailing services and sites built for this purpose.

An alternative, and often more elegant, solution, made possible by the technology of our times, is to avoid this entire ordeal and build a wedding website. If you or someone you know is knowledgeable in building websites (which is a simple process today with platforms like WordPress, free domain registrars, one-click website building options etc.), then it's far easier to build a beautiful, interactive, personalized website with gorgeous photographs of you and your partner.

You could use it to compile a registry, send invitations and save-the-dates with links leading back to the site (where your guests could R.S.V.P. immediately, as well as selecting any food preferences, etc. which you need them to), as well as start a personalized Twitter-ish feed, or uploading videos if you want to keep everyone abreast of everything that's happening behind-the-scenes. The possibilities here are quite endless.

Even if no one that you're personally acquainted with could do this for you, you can easily hire freelance web-designers on competitive job platforms like oDesk. Elance etc. to do this for you without breaking a sweat.

In the case of party favors, it's often noted in retrospect by married couples that they could have done away with them altogether. Party favors usually end up tossed away, and just add up to another pointless expense that most guests wouldn't even miss when they're having a great time at your wedding.

If you aren't building a website of your own, you can use websites like myregistry.com and simpleregistry.com to build an online registry for your wedding gifts.

However, there's another alternative you could keep in mind here. Wedding gifts in the form of cash are not uncommon. It may be helpful for you, since you're planning your wedding on a tight budget, to abstain from receiving material gifts and ask for cash instead that you could then use on your honeymoon, to re-build your savings, etc.

If you fear that would be impolite, you could simply word it in a way that would be more palatable for you.

An oft-used direction seems to include sending a message to everyone invited saying that since you and your partner have all the material items you need to comfortably settle into marital life together, you aren't accepting any gifts for your wedding. But, since the two of you are hoping to go somewhere exotic and beautiful for your honeymoon, you're starting a honeymoon fund. Anyone still wishing to gift the two of you is more than welcome to make a donation to it for that purpose.

Lastly, the alternate options for officiants in weddings have now become quite well-known. You can ask someone you're close with to register themselves online as a wedding officiant to conduct your ceremony. It may also save you money that venues might charge for bringing in their own officiants.

Conclusion

While I'm positive that you'll pick up more tips to ease your way through this process, I hope that this guide has provided you with enough new information, directions and points-of-view for you to now feel confident going out and making your dream come true on a shoestring budget. Don't limit yourselves to what everyone else has been doing, instead forge a fresh path right from the start. I can promise you that your wedding will be far more memorable, far less generic, and the talk of your near and dear ones for decades to come.

Beyond that, I would just like to take a moment to remind you of the importance of your partner, over and above your wedding day. Cherish each other's thoughts and opinions, as if each word from the other's tongue were a diamond. Always gaze upon each other as if the other were a seven-course feast, and you were starving for them. Take some time out of the hectic schedules of your jobs, wedding preparations and so on to just spend some time in each other's company, watch a movie together, go bowling, or whatever you like. Remember that the two of you have made it this far through thick and thin, through the ups and downs of life, and each trial and tribulation that you have conquered together. Life is crazy, planning a wedding is not. It's a walk through a beautiful, moon-lit, rose-garden in spring, by comparison.

Keep your cool with each other through the most panicky of times and you'll get through to the other side happier than ever, as partners bound together for life.

Last, I'd like to thank you for purchasing this book! If you enjoyed it or found it helpful, I'd greatly appreciate it if you'd take a moment to leave a review on Amazon. Thank you! And congratulations, and I wish you all the best for a very happy and prosperous married life!

Made in the USA
Middletown, DE
14 December 2021

55768266R00038